CRAFTS · FROM · THE · PAST

The
AZTECS

D1404564

CRAFTS · FROM · THE · PAST

The AZTECS

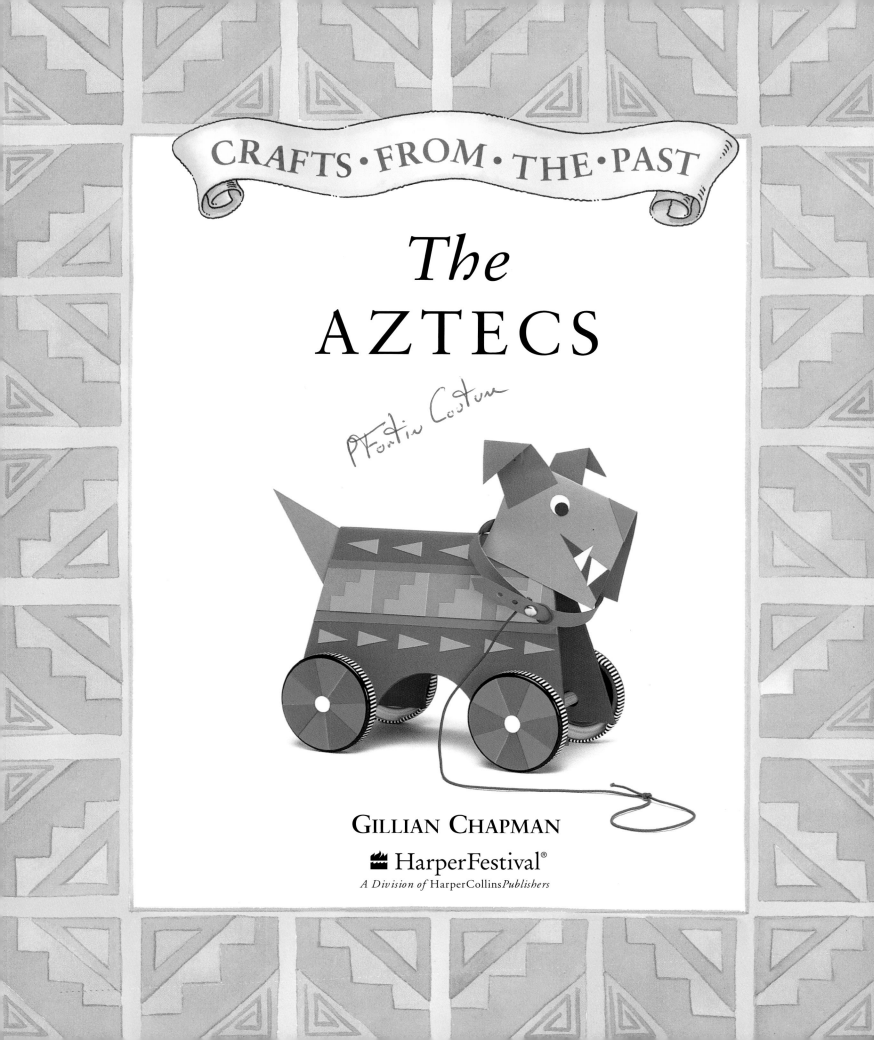

GILLIAN CHAPMAN

HarperFestival®
A Division of HarperCollinsPublishers

GENERAL CRAFT TIPS AND SAFETY PRECAUTIONS

Read the instructions carefully, then gather everything you'll need before you begin to work.

It will help if you plan your design first on scrap paper.

If you are working with papier-mâché or paint, cover the work surfaces with newspaper.

Always use a cutting mat when cutting with a mat knife and ask an adult to help if you are using sharp tools.

Keep paint and glue brushes separate and always wash them out after use.

Don't be impatient—make sure the plaster is set, and the papier-mâché or paint is thoroughly dry before moving on to the next step!

All the projects make perfect presents!
Try to make them as carefully as you can.

RECYCLING

Start collecting materials for craftwork. Save newspaper, colored paper and cardboard, cardboard boxes and tubes of different sizes, magazines, gift wrap, and scraps of string and ribbon.

Clean plastic containers and old utensils are perfect for mixing plaster and making paper pulp.

HarperCollins®, 🏭®, and HarperFestival® are registered trademarks of HarperCollins Publishers Inc.

Copyright © 1997 by Fernleigh Books
First published in the United States in hardcover by Heinemann Interactive Library, an imprint of Reed Educational & Professional Publishing, 1350 East Touhy Avenue, Suite 240 West, Des Plaines, Illinois 60018

Produced by Fernleigh Books
Designer—Gail Rose; Photographer—Rupert Horrox;
Illustrator—Teri Gower;
Picture researcher—Jennie Karrach
Printed in Hong Kong by Wing King Tong Co. Ltd.

Library of Congress Cataloging-in-Publication Data

Chapman, Gillian.
The Aztecs / by Gillian Chapman.
p. cm. —(Crafts from the past)
Summary: Projects based on various features of Aztec culture recreate some of their arts and crafts, including woven textiles, mosaic masks, jewelry, featherwork, and wheeled toys.
ISBN 0-688-17748-4
1. Handicraft—Mexico—Juvenile literature. 2. Indian craft—Juvenile literature. 3. Aztecs—Juvenile literature.
[1. Indian craft. 2. Handicraft. 3. Aztecs. 4. Indians of Mexico.]
I. Title. II. Series.
TT28.C43 2000
972'.018 21—dc21   99-042373

First HarperFestival edition, 2000
10 9 8 7 6 5 4 3 2 1

Visit us on the world Wide Web!
http://www.harperchildrens.com

Bodleian Library: top and 24; British Museum: 18; Michael Holford: 30; Museum fur Volkerkunde: 22; Odyssey Productions: 20; Reed Educational & Professional Publishing: 14; The Saint Louis Art Museum: 28; N.J. Saunders: 6 top and bottom; South American Pictures: 34 © Tony Morrison; Werner Forman Archive: 7 top, and 7 bottom © Museum fur Volkerkunde, 8 middle, 32 and 36 © National Museum of Anthropology, Mexico City, 8 bottom, 10, and 16 © British Museum, 26 © Pigorini Museum of Prehistory and Ethnography, Rome

Acknowledgments
Every effort has been made to contact copyright holders of any material reproduced in this book.
Any omissions will be rectified in subsequent printings if notice is given to the publisher.

Some words are shown in **bold,** like this.
You can find out what they mean by looking in the glossary.
The glossary also helps you say difficult words.

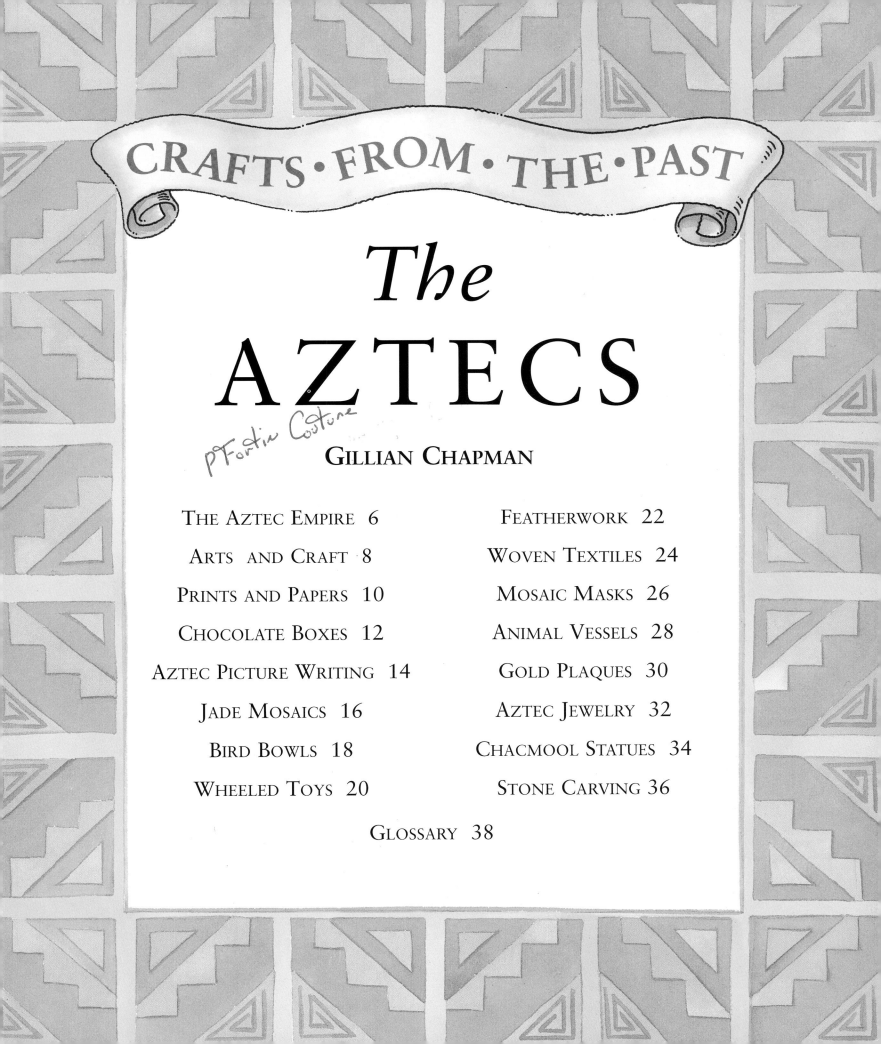

CRAFTS · FROM · THE · PAST

The AZTECS

P Fortin Costume

GILLIAN CHAPMAN

THE AZTEC EMPIRE

THE AZTECS were originally a small **nomadic** tribe who first settled in the Valley of Mexico in early 1300. Gradually they began to prosper and eventually conquered much of the surrounding area, taking over land from neighboring tribes.

At its peak the Aztec Empire contained over 15 million people, living in 500 towns and cities. Some of these cities were larger than European cities of the time. When the Spanish first arrived, the empire stretched across Mexico from the Atlantic to the Pacific.

The Aztecs were a tough people. They lived in a hot, barren land and were constantly at war. They believed in powerful gods that had to be kept content with human **sacrifice.** Otherwise, the gods would become angry and destroy their world with earthquakes and drought.

Prisoners were taken from conquered cities, together with **tribute** that was paid to the Aztecs to prevent further attack. This system kept the Aztecs rich. At the time of the Spanish invasion they were sacrificing over 20,000 people a year.

TOP. *Stone walls in the Oaxaca Valley decorated with Aztec step designs.*

ABOVE. *Serpent head carved from stone.*

SUPERSTITION AND PROPHECY

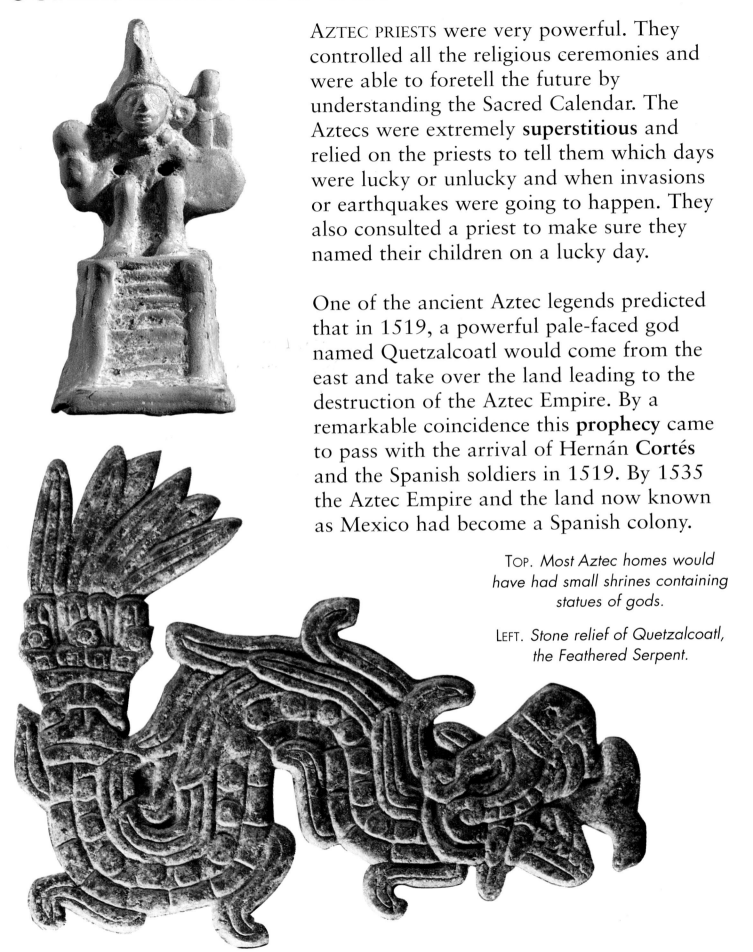

AZTEC PRIESTS were very powerful. They controlled all the religious ceremonies and were able to foretell the future by understanding the Sacred Calendar. The Aztecs were extremely **superstitious** and relied on the priests to tell them which days were lucky or unlucky and when invasions or earthquakes were going to happen. They also consulted a priest to make sure they named their children on a lucky day.

One of the ancient Aztec legends predicted that in 1519, a powerful pale-faced god named Quetzalcoatl would come from the east and take over the land leading to the destruction of the Aztec Empire. By a remarkable coincidence this **prophecy** came to pass with the arrival of Hernán **Cortés** and the Spanish soldiers in 1519. By 1535 the Aztec Empire and the land now known as Mexico had become a Spanish colony.

TOP. *Most Aztec homes would have had small shrines containing statues of gods.*

LEFT. *Stone relief of Quetzalcoatl, the Feathered Serpent.*

ARTS AND CRAFT

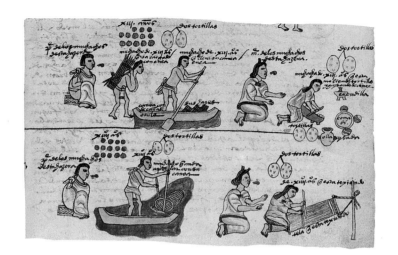

AZTEC PEASANTS made everything they needed from the natural materials they found. Clay was molded into pots and baked in the sun. Reeds were woven into baskets, and cactus fibers were spun into thread to make cloth, fishing nets, and rope. They also brought goods into the city markets to trade.

As the empire grew, the Aztecs traded with different tribes and discovered new materials and skills. They also took over large areas of land, and the arts and crafts of the conquered peoples became part of the Aztec style.

Large quantities of **tribute** was paid to the Aztecs in gold, feathers, animal skins, and anything of value. Tribute also included crafted items of woven cloth, jewelry, and pottery. Aztec craftworkers were influenced by the patterns and designs that came from other cultures.

Craftworkers were organized into **guilds**, and the skills and trade secrets of particular crafts passed down from father to son. Whole families worked together to make a particular item like a feather shield (see page 22) or decorated cloak for a warrior.

TOP. *Drawings from a codex page show scenes of daily life.*

FAR RIGHT. *A gold earring made by Mixtec craftsmen.*

RIGHT. *Wooden drum decorated with owl carving.*

AZTEC CRAFT TIPS

There are many similarities between these projects and the craft techniques used by the Aztecs. Before starting a project, look carefully at the Aztec crafts and try to use similar colors and designs.

To decorate some Aztec projects, it is easier to make a design from scraps of colored paper glued onto the surface, than it is to use paint. Colored stickers can also make very colorful patterns.

If you are using materials, such as, a pack of feathers to decorate a project – sort them into piles of different colors. Try to use the colors in the best way possible to make your designs interesting.

Simple materials, such as colored paper and gift wrap, can be used to decorate the Aztec projects.

With the mosaic projects, use cut-up colored pictures from magazines or scraps of gift wrap to make the mosaic pieces. Choose papers to give you the correct range of colors – blues, greens, and turquoise.

To decorate projects with colored papers and mosaic pieces, first plan your design by arranging the pieces on the surface. When you are happy with the design, glue the pieces into position using a glue stick.

White glue is very useful for gluing cardboard, string, and collage materials like those used to make the Gold Plaques and the Aztec jewelry. It can be diluted with water to make papier-mâché and paper pulp.

9

PRINTS AND PAPERS

Aztec patterns are basically very simple. It is the way the designs are repeated in rows that makes them so effective and perfect for print designs.

THE AZTECS decorated their textiles and metalwork with distinctive patterns. Bands of repeating geometric designs and stylized animal shapes were painted or carved onto their pottery. **Abstract** patterns of zig-zag and stepped lines were most typical, usually painted in two colors.

Small carved **relief** blocks made from clay were used to stamp patterns onto fabric. This type of stamp was also used to paint the faces of dancers at **festival** time.

DESIGNING PATTERNS

YOU WILL NEED
Scrap paper — Brush or roller
Felt-tip pens & pencil — Mat knife
Newspaper — Paper &
Thick paints & tray — cardboard
Printing block — Potato, soft eraser, or styrofoam
Ask an adult to help you cut out the printing block.

1. Look at the Aztec patterns on this page and pages 6–7. Sketch some designs of your own on scrap paper, using one or two colors.

2. Keep your ideas simple and design them within a square or rectangular framework. Color them in different ways to see which colors work best.

3. Either copy your design three or four times and see how it looks when repeated in a row, or if you can, photocopy it.

MAKING PRINTS

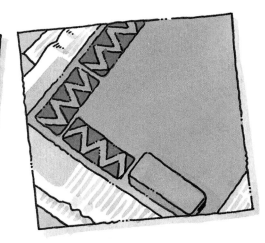

1. Simple designs are the most effective. Cut a potato in half. Draw the pattern on the surface of one half and cut it out carefully with a mat knife. Ask an adult to help you.

2. Small blocks of styrofoam packing or soft erasers also make good printing blocks. Draw the design on the flat surface and carefully cut it out with a mat knife.

3. Cover the work surface with newspaper. Dip the printing block into paint (alternatively, brush or roller over the printing surface), then press it firmly onto the paper.

Use the printing blocks to decorate your own Aztec cards, wrapping paper, tags, and bookmarks.

Printing designs onto a contrasting colored paper can create a nice effect.

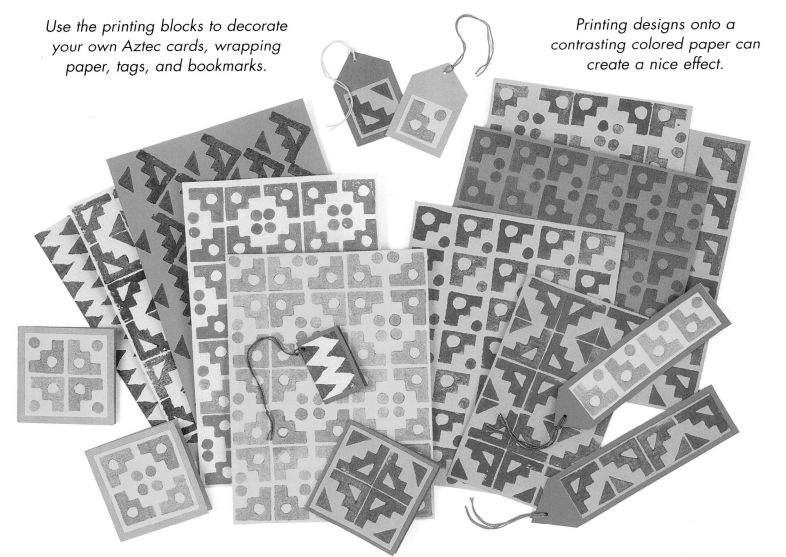

CHOCOLATE BOXES

AZTEC WORKERS and farmers lived on a very simple diet of corn, vegetables, and fruit. The corn was ground into flour to make **"tortillas"**, flat pancakes, eaten at every meal. Wealthier people ate exotic foods like spices, pineapples, and seafood, which were all brought into the cities from warmer climates.

Today chocolate is still a luxury, although we can all afford to buy it. Try making some special Aztec gift boxes to put chocolates in. Stacked together they look like an Aztec temple! Aztecs held **festivals** at stepped temples like the one in the photograph above.

Rich and noble families also enjoyed a type of chocolate "milkshake" made from ground cocoa beans mixed with water. The frothy mixture was sweetened with honey and vanilla.

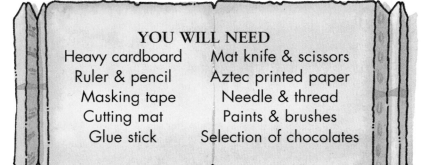

YOU WILL NEED
Heavy cardboard	Mat knife & scissors
Ruler & pencil	Aztec printed paper
Masking tape	Needle & thread
Cutting mat	Paints & brushes
Glue stick	Selection of chocolates

AZTEC BOX

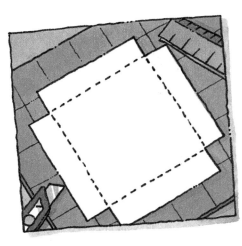

1. Draw a square in the center of the heavy cardboard. This will be the base of the box. Then draw in the sides. Cut the shape out carefully.

2. Score along the four sides using the scissors, and fold them up. Secure the sides with pieces of masking tape to form a box.

3. Cut out a square piece of cardboard, 1/4 in. larger than the base, and tape it to one edge. Paint the box inside and out and leave to dry.

4. Make some printed paper with an Aztec design (see pages 10–11). Cut a printed strip the same depth as the box and stick it around the outside of the box using the glue stick.

5. Cut out a printed square the same size as the lid and glue it on the lid. Make a tassel, thread it through the lid and secure it with tape. Cover the inside of the lid with a square of printed paper.

Make a set of Aztec boxes – all different sizes.

TASSEL MAKING

1. Wind a long length of thread around a piece of cardboard.
2. Tie the threads together at the top and remove the cardboard.
3. Wind some thread around the tassel, secure it with a knot, then cut through the ends.

Cover a plain box of chocolates with Aztec paper to make it extra special!

AZTEC PICTURE WRITING

THE AZTECS developed a very complex system of picture writing. Each picture, or **"glyph"**, represented an object or idea. Groups of glyphs made a larger picture story. It was a sophisticated system that only **scribes** and priests could interpret.

The Aztecs kept records of every aspect of their lives – payment of **tribute,** conquests in war, and domestic details. They believed in **prophecies** and avoided the unlucky days on their calendars.

They recorded information in large zig-zag books, called **"codices"**, made from **bark paper** or animal skin.

ZIG-ZAG CODEX

1. Tape the first two pages together, leaving a 1/4 in. gap between them. Neatly fold over the ends of the tape.

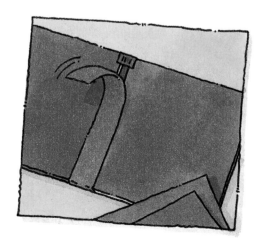

2. Cover the gap with a length of tape. Add pages until the codex is the right length for your story.

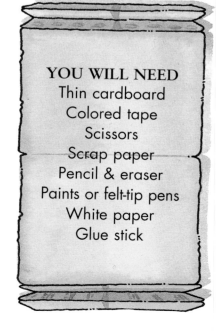

YOU WILL NEED
Thin cardboard
Colored tape
Scissors
Scrap paper
Pencil & eraser
Paints or felt-tip pens
White paper
Glue stick

14

PICTURE STORY

1. Aztec glyphs are very similar to cartoon strips. The story can be understood by looking at the pictures. Make up a short story and tell it as a series of glyphs.

2. Work out your story on scrap paper. You may prefer to draw the pictures on paper, color them in, cut them out, and then stick them into the codex.

3. The Aztecs showed speech as a tongue symbol coming out of a mouth, like a small speech bubble. A line of footprints indicated a journey.

This picture story tells the adventures of a group of friends on vacation together.

The Aztecs used glyphs to represent names, dates, and ideas. Try thinking up glyphs to make your story really interesting!

JADE MOSAICS

YOU WILL NEED
Modeling clay
Newspaper
White glue & brush
Magazine pictures –
blue, turquoise,
green & orange
Scissors
Craft knife
Black paint & brush
Scraps of white card
Pipe cleaners

THE AZTECS loved precious stones and crafted them into magnificent statues, jewelry, masks and **sacrificial** objects. Green stones, like jade, turquoise, and malachite, were particularly valued. Jade was the most precious as it symbolized water, the life-giving force.

Carved wooden shapes like this serpent were covered with pieces of stone or shell. Ceremonial death masks were made from a real skull, complete with teeth, and decorated with turquoise and shell **mosaics**.

TURQUOISE SERPENT

1. Take the clay and roll it into a long sausage shape. Use it to make the serpent's body. Then mold two heads and attach them to both ends.

2. Use diluted white glue to cover the clay mold with six layers of newspaper strips. Use small paper pieces to cover the curves and corners. Leave to dry.

3. Remove the clay. Trim the edge of the shape with scissors. Carefully cut out the eye holes with a mat knife. Then paint the serpent black.

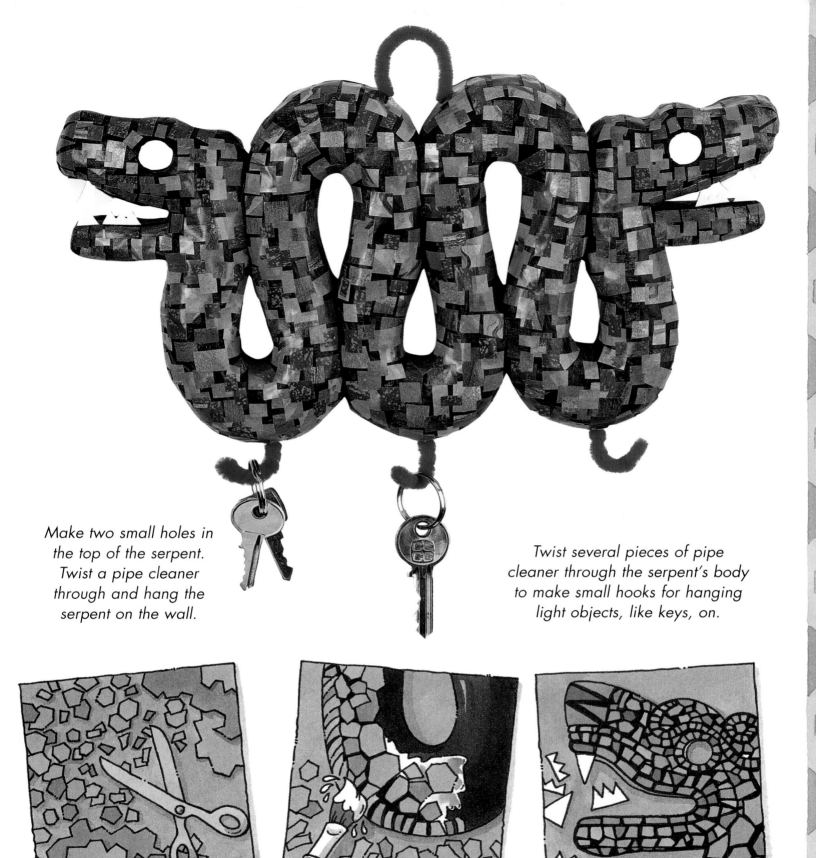

Make two small holes in the top of the serpent. Twist a pipe cleaner through and hang the serpent on the wall.

Twist several pieces of pipe cleaner through the serpent's body to make small hooks for hanging light objects, like keys, on.

4. Cut up the turquoise, blue, and green pictures into small pieces. The more shades of blue you can find, the better the finished mosaic will be.

5. Glue the pieces to the serpent. Look carefully at the photograph of the Aztec serpent and see how they used mosaic pieces of different sizes to great effect.

6. Complete the design by adding the nose and mouth details in orange pieces. Cut out teeth shapes from white cardboard and glue in place.

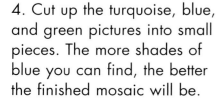

BIRD BOWLS

AZTEC POTTERY was shaped by hand without using a potter's wheel. Some pots have carved animal forms. Others are painted with detailed scenes from Aztec legends. Some are decorated inside and out with **abstract** patterns and designs (see page 10).

The Aztecs left no written records, so much can be learned about their history and culture from the picture stories painted on their pottery.

YOU WILL NEED

Newspaper	Modeling clay
Large & small bowl	Mat knife
with similar size bases	Scissors
White glue & brush	White poster paint
Cooking oil	Poster paints & brush
saran wrap	Clear varnish & brush

BIRD BOWLS

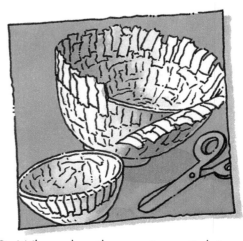

1. Coat the inside and rims of both bowls with cooking oil and completely cover with saran wrap. Use a diluted white glue and cover the bowls with six layers of newspaper strips.

2. Make a bird shape from modeling clay and cover it with several layers of small newspaper strips. Then leave the bowls and bird shape to dry for at least two days.

3. When dry, the papier–mâché shapes should come away easily from the bowls. Remove the saran wrap and trim the edges. Paste two layers of small strips over the trimmed edges and leave to dry.

The cup was made in the same way as the bowl. It has a parrot shaped handle and wooden beads sewn through the rim.

4. Carefully cut the paper bird shape in half with a mat knife and remove the modeling clay. Then glue the two halves together with small strips of paper.

5. Join the bowls together with white glue. Paste strips of paper across where they join. Stick the bird to the rim of the bowl with glued strips of paper.

6. Paint the bird bowl with two coats of white paint, allowing each coat to dry. Then paint on an Aztec design. Finally, varnish the bowl to protect it.

WHEELED TOYS

THE AZTECS did not realize that the wheel was very useful. They had no wheeled carts or wagons for transporting heavy loads, and they made all their pottery without a potter's wheel. But they made wheeled toy animals to amuse their children!

Animals played a part in domestic life and religious rituals. Dogs were trained for hunting, and some were bred for meat. Wild cats, like the jaguar, were worshiped for their power and strength.

Wheeled animals, like the carved toy dog shown in the photograph above, have been found in Aztec graves. The Aztecs believed that a wheeled dog would guide its master's soul to a final resting place.

WHEELED DOG

YOU WILL NEED

Stiff cardboard	Two 6 in. lengths
Sharp pencil	of dowel
Scissors	Paints & brush
Four thumbtacks	White glue & brush
Four plastic lids,	Ask an adult to help you
the same size	make the wheels.

1. Fold the cardboard in half. In pencil, draw a simple animal body shape. Cut out the shape, cutting through both thicknesses of cardboard, but not along the fold.

2. Mark where the wheel holes should go on the folded shape. Carefully pierce through the cardboard using a sharp pencil. Make sure each pair of holes lines up.

3. Fold a small piece of cardboard and draw the shape of an animal head onto it. Cut the animal head shape out and glue it to the body shape using white glue.

4. Decorate the folded shape to make it look like an animal. Aztec pottery and toy animals have stylized markings. Look at the designs on this page and pages 8–11. You may choose to use one of these patterns on your animal.

5. Glue decorated circles of cardboard onto the four lids and leave to dry. Carefully make a small hole in the center of each lid by pushing a thumbtack through each one. You may need an adult's help.

6. Attach one lid to a length of dowel with a thumbtack. Thread the dowel through the holes, then pin another lid to the other end. Repeat for the second wheel axle. Make sure the dowels both turn easily in the holes.

Glue extra features, such as cardboard ears and a tail to the animals.

Make a collar and leash so your animal can guide you along!

FEATHERWORK

FEATHERWORK was a highly skilled craft. Spectacular clothing, such as, capes and headdresses, were made for emperors and high priests. Warriors wore feathered tunics and helmets – the higher the rank, the more elaborate the decoration. They carried leather shields (left) patterned with feather designs.

Tropical birds were hunted for their colored feathers, but they were also bred in huge aviaries. **Quetzal** birds were prized for their beautiful plumage.

The Aztecs drew their designs onto cloth, then glued or sewed on feathers. Try making these feather **mosaics** on a shield or fan using the same Aztec techniques.

FEATHER SHIELD

YOU WILL NEED

Large & small circles of heavy cardboard	Pack of colored craft feathers
Strips of cardboard	Colored
Scotch tape	cardboard scraps
White glue & brush	Paper & pencil
Scissors	Small stick handles

1. Draw the shield design on paper, then transfer it to the circle of heavy cardboard. Sort the craft feathers into piles of different colors.

2. Start at the outer edge of the shield and work in towards the center. Glue a small area of the cardboard and begin to cover it with feathers.

3. Following your design, overlap the feathers in layers, until the cardboard is completely covered. Use the colors in interesting ways.

4. Make a circle pattern from the scraps of colored cardboard. Glue it to the shield to complete the design.

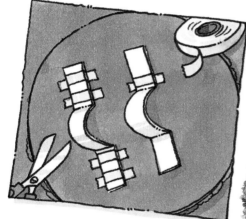

5. Finally, tape strips of cardboard to the back of the shield. Use these as grips for holding the shield.

The feather fans are made in the same way as the shield, only using smaller circles of cardboard.

Decorate a small stick and tape it to the back of the fan to use as a handle.

WOVEN TEXTILES

Aztec girls learned to weave at home. The picture above, taken from an Aztec **codex,** shows a mother teaching her daughter to weave. Aztec clothes were loose, simple, and had no pockets so people probably carried small bags similar to the one on the far right. Why not weave your own bag!

TEXTILES were extremely important in Aztec society. Vast quantities of textiles were offered to the gods and beautiful hangings decorated temples and were worn for religious processions.

The Aztecs did not keep sheep. Instead, they spun and dyed cotton and plant fibers. They then wove them into fabric using a **"back-strap" loom.** People wore clothing that reflected their social class, but merchants wore plain cloaks of cactus fiber to hide their wealthy status.

YOU WILL NEED
Stiff cardboard
Scissors
Long blunt needle
Balls of colored yarns
Felt for lining the bag
Ruler

WOVEN BAG

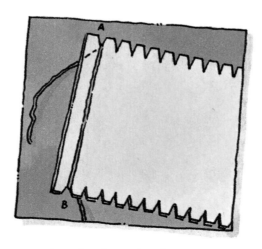

1. Remember, the finished bag will be the same size as the cardboard! Cut the same number of notches, 1/2 in. apart, along the top and bottom.

2. Wind a length of strong yarn around the notches as shown. Secure the yarn into notch A, then wind it around the card into notch B.

3. Wind the yarn back into notch A, and then across into notch C. Then wind the yarn behind the card to notch D and take the yarn back to notch C.

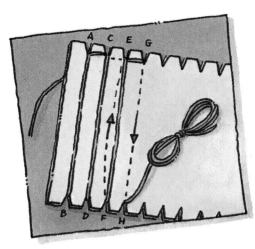
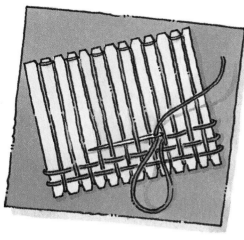
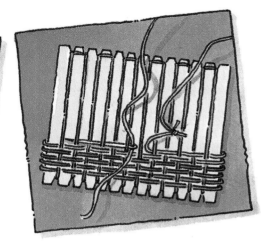

4. Take the yarn behind the cardboard into E and down to F. From here, the yarn goes back to E, across into G, and down to H. Continue following this sequence around all the notches. Secure both ends.

5. Thread a needle with a long length of yarn and weave it though the threads, in and out across the front, then across the back. Continue in this way, weaving around the cardboard.

6. Tie on new lengths of yarn as needed and continue weaving lengths around the cardboard until it is completely covered. Use many different colors to make a bright bag.

7. Fasten the ends of the yarn. Carefully slip the loops over the top notches of the card-board, loosen the weaving from the bottom notches, then gently slide the card out.

Give the bag a braided handle and decorate it with colored tassels (see page 13). Line it with some colored felt.

MOSAIC MASKS

Masks played an important role in all Aztec **festivals**. Large stone masks were too heavy to be worn, but were used as temple decorations. During religious ceremonies, they were made to represent the gods, attached to wooden frames, and draped in elaborate costumes.

Burial masks often have very realistic portraits of Aztec faces. They were sculpted from special pieces of greenstone or granite, with eyes and teeth inlaid in shell. But the most spectacular Aztec masks were made with **mosaics**.

Craftworkers skillfully covered wooden masks or even skulls with tiny pieces of turquoise, jade, and precious stones.

MOSAIC MASK

YOU WILL NEED
Paper & felt-tip pens   White glue & brush
Ruler   Magazine pictures
Modeling clay   for mosaic work
Board   Scissors
Newspaper   Thin black elastic
Mat knife   Black paint & brush

1. First you will need to make a life-size sketch of a mask on paper. Either copy the ideas shown here, or create your own design.

2. Take the modeling clay and place it on a board. Follow your design and roughly mold the clay into the mask shape, checking the size with a ruler.

3. When the mask is the right size, add more clay to build up the features, such as, the forehead, cheeks, and nose. Keep the clay surface smooth.

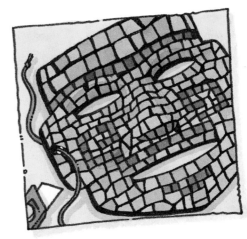

4. Use a diluted white glue to cover the mold with six layers of newspaper strips. Try to apply the paper evenly using small pieces to cover all the curves and corners.

5. When the mask is dry, carefully remove all the clay. Trim around the edge of the mask with scissors and cut out the eyes and mouth with a mat knife.

6. Paint the mask black. Cut the magazine pictures into pieces and use them to make the mosaic pattern. Decorate the mask using the mosaic techniques on page 17.

Make holes in the mask and thread elastic through so you can either wear the mask or hang it on the wall.

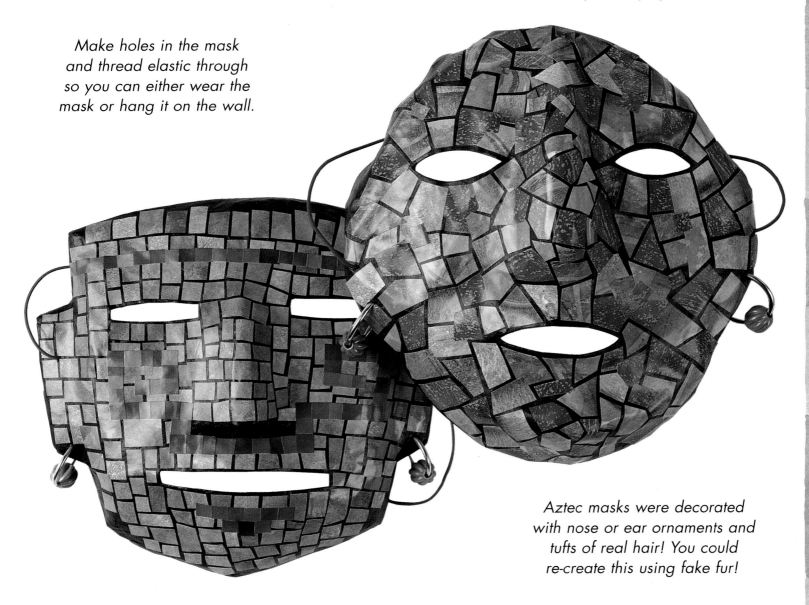

Aztec masks were decorated with nose or ear ornaments and tufts of real hair! You could re-create this using fake fur!

27

ANIMAL VESSELS

THE FINEST and most decorative Aztec pottery was used exclusively by the rich or by priests during special rituals. Pots used everyday were very plain and simple, but all plates and bowls were shaped by hand.

Potters also made some very unusual vessels in the shape of birds and animals, such as, dogs. The Aztecs kept dogs as pets and companions and believed they would guide them through the afterlife.

Dog bones are commonly found in Aztec graves. They were probably buried next to their masters, along with dog shaped vessels, like the one above.

DOG VESSEL

YOU WILL NEED

Newspaper
Two large bowls
Hot water
(*Pulp will need to soak overnight)

Clean empty container, cardboard or tin
White glue & brush
Poster paint & brush
Clear varnish

1. To make the paper pulp, tear up newspaper into small pieces and put them in a large bowl. Cover the paper pieces with hot water and leave them to soak overnight.

2. Take handfuls of paper, squeeze out all the water and place it in the second bowl. Then, using your hands, blend it together with white glue until it feels soft and smooth.

3. Press small lumps of pulp to the sides of the container and work all the way around, building up the animal shape. Brush on extra white glue to help the pulp stick to the sides.

Try making an unusual vessel in the shape of your favorite animal and use it to keep your desk neat.

4. Pulp is very easy to model with your fingers. Make the large body and head shapes first by pressing the pulp firmly together. Add more pulp to make the ears, paws, and tail.

5. Gently rub over the surface with your fingers to make it smooth and remove any lumps. Then put the dog vessel in a safe place and leave it to thoroughly dry.

6. Paint the container inside and out and let it dry. Use either natural clay colors or bright colorful patterns. Then apply two coats of clear varnish to protect it.

GOLD PLAQUES

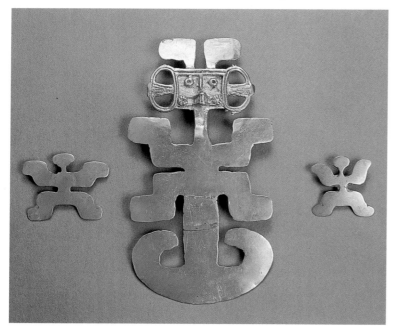

THE AZTECS were famous for their gold jewelry and metalwork, but few pieces survive today. Much was taken back to Spain by the **Conquistadors** and melted down to make gold bars. Aztec goldsmiths were very skilled and held high status in society. They produced elaborate jewelry, lip and nose plugs, masks and pendants, as well as spectacular golden temple decorations.

The golden plaque designs on this page are based on these stylized Tolima figures (above) made from beaten gold. Make an Aztec gold plaque to hang on the wall.

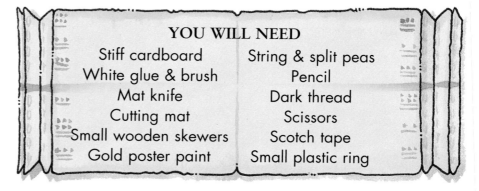

YOU WILL NEED

Stiff cardboard	String & split peas
White glue & brush	Pencil
Mat knife	Dark thread
Cutting mat	Scissors
Small wooden skewers	Scotch tape
Gold poster paint	Small plastic ring

GOLDEN PLAQUE

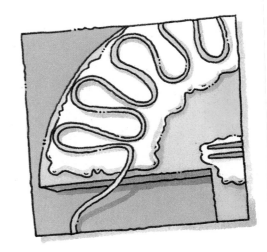

1. Copy the plaque outline on to the cardboard and draw in the pattern. Use the mat knife to cut out the cardboard shape.

2. Spread a thin layer of glue over part of the cardboard. Glue pieces of skewer, string, and split peas to the design.

3. Continue to build up a raised pattern over the whole plaque, making sure all the pieces are stuck down firmly.

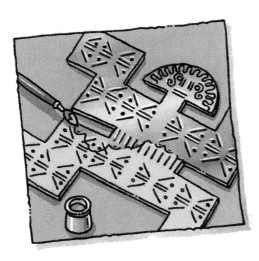

4. Leave somewhere safe and let the glue dry. When the glue is dry, paint the plaque with gold poster paint.

5. Cut out four circles of cardboard and paint them gold. Hang them from the head with thread, taped to the back.

6. Glue a small plastic ring to the back of the plaque and use it to hang the plaque on the wall.

Make these colorful plaques of Aztec gold to hang on the wall.

To make the gold plaque look really old, dab it with bronze paint.

AZTEC JEWELRY

WHEN THE SPANISH **CONQUISTADORS** entered **Tenochtitlan** in 1519, they were amazed at the wealth of the Aztecs. The Emperor **Montezuma** believed, because of a **prophecy,** that the Spanish leader was a god. He showered **Cortés** with gifts of gold and beautiful jewelry.

The Spanish became greedy and in the conflict that followed, they plundered all the Aztecs' treasure. It was taken back to Spain, where all the spectacular gold jewelry and decorations were melted down.

A few pieces survived, like this turquoise and gold brooch. Try and re-create some Aztec jewelry using these **mosaic** designs.

MOSAIC MEDALLIONS

YOU WILL NEED

Pencil & stiff cardboard	Fine string or cord
Compass	Gold beads
Scissors	Needle & thread
Turquoise paper scraps	Safety pin
Glue stick	Scotch tape
White glue & brush	Hole punch
Gold poster paint & brush	

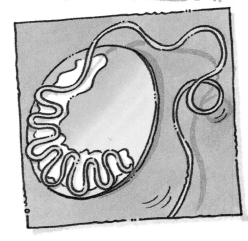

1. To make the simple medallion shape, draw a circle on the cardboard with the compass. Carefully cut out the circle with scissors and paint it gold.

2. Cut the turquoise paper scraps into small pieces. Arrange these on the gold circle to make the mosaic design, then stick them in place with the glue stick.

3. To make a more detailed medallion, first glue a length of curled string around the edge of the circle using white glue. Paint it gold and complete the mosaic in the center.

32

PENDANTS AND BROOCHES

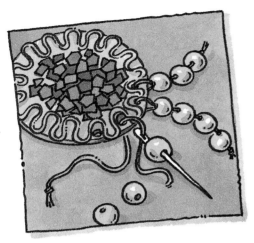

1. Punch four small holes along the bottom edge of a medallion and attach strings of gold beads. Tape a safety pin to the back of the cardboard to make a brooch.

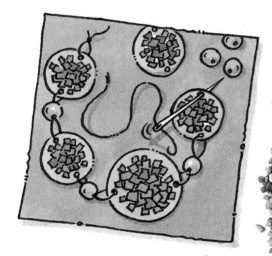

2. Try making a number of medallions of different sizes and designs. The pendant and necklace are made by making holes in several medallions and threading them together with the gold beads.

The mosaic pendant shown here re-creates the Aztec brooch design opposite.

CHACMOOL STATUES

THE AZTECS worshiped many gods and making offerings to them was an important part of their religion. They believed these offerings pleased the gods and kept the sun alive, ensuring their crops would grow and people would not starve.

Aztec priests regularly made offerings on the altars at the tops of the temple pyramids, such as the great temple shown on page 12. Inside the temple, reclining stone figures called **chacmools** represented the god's messengers.

These reclining figures were carved out of stone and held an offering bowl up to the skies. Offerings to the sun were placed in their laps.

CHACMOOL BOOKENDS

YOU WILL NEED

Pairs of boxes (see Step 1)	Paints & brush
White glue & brush	Colored paper scraps
Sand or small stones (to weight the bookends)	Pencil & felt-tip pens
	Scissors
Scotch tape	Glue stick
	Pairs of plastic lids

1. To make one bookend, you will need two boxes. One twice as long as the other, but both of similar widths. They will be glued together to make the bookend shape.

2. Fill the larger box with sand or gravel, and seal it closed with plenty of tape. Tape up the smaller box and glue them both together using white glue.

3. Repeat this process with the other boxes, so you have two bookend shapes. Paint the boxes to cover up the strips of tape and any printing on the surfaces.

This pair of Chacmools are fun to make, and are also perfect bookends.

The lids on their laps make handy containers for paper clips, coins, and other small treasures.

4. Decorate the front of the bookends with colored paper shapes. Carefully cut out a simple chacmool figure from paper and glue one to the front of each bookend.

5. To decorate the sides and top of each bookend, cut out some paper shapes and glue them together to make colorful patterns. Or color the surfaces with felt-tip pen designs.

6. Glue a plastic lid on the top of each chacmool using white glue – they make attractive hats! A second upturned lid glued to the body makes a handy container.

STONE CARVING

THE AZTEC CITY of **Tenochtitlan** became the most powerful city in Mexico. It was home for 100,000 people, a great trading center, and was well planned on a grid system of streets and **causeways.**

The Aztecs created the city with many practical amenities such as canals, aqueducts, and reservoirs. They also built impressive stone buildings – palaces, temples, and **ball courts,** which were richly decorated with carved stone friezes (see page 6). As religion and mythology were central to Aztec life, these carvings depicted the legends of the gods and would originally have been brightly painted. Try painting your Aztec tile in bright oranges, reds, and yellows.

The largest known Aztec sculpture is a circular stone relief known as the Sun Stone, or Calendar. The Aztecs were very **superstitious** and consulted the calendar to make horoscopes and **prophecies.**

CARVED TILE

1. Draw a design for the tile on tracing paper. Keep your ideas simple and try copying a figure or pattern from the Aztec carving shown above.

2. Measure the design and make a cardboard mold the same size, with sides 2 in. deep. Fold up the sides and fasten them with tape.

3. Following the instructions on the packet, mix up some plaster and pour it into the mold to a depth of 1 1/4 in. Smooth the surface and let it dry.

YOU WILL NEED

Tracing paper & pencil   Scotch tape
Heavy cardboard   Paints & brush
Ruler   Newspapers
Cutting mat & mat knife   Nail or carving tool
Plaster, an old plastic container
& mixing utensils

4. Make sure the plaster is dry. Remove it from the mold. Choose the smooth side to work on, and paint the surface with a thick coat of paint.

Try painting the tile several different colors to give it a more interesting finish, then let it dry.

5. Trace your design onto the painted surface so an impression is left on the paint. Then carefully scratch out the line using a sharp nail or carving tool.

If you scratch out a line by mistake just paint it over with some paint of the same color!

GLOSSARY

Abstract – design or pattern made from shapes with no recognizable forms

Artifact – object or work of art made by craftworkers

Back-strap loom – simple loom used to weave cloth; one end is fixed to a tree or post, with the other supported by a strap around the weaver's waist

Ball courts – huge walled courtyards, over 100 yards long, decorated with stone carvings and statues, where ball games were played

Bark paper – paper material used to make codices, made from the bark of the wild fig tree

Causeway – raised pathway crossing a flooded area

Chacmool – large reclining stone figure found in the temple, representing a messenger of the gods; offerings were placed in their laps as food for the gods

Codex – zig-zag book, made from bark paper or parchment, illustrated with glyphs; many codices contain information about Aztec conquests, records of tribute and details of daily life, religious beliefs, and prophecies

Conquistadors – Spanish explorers and soldiers who travelled to Tenochtitlan in the 16th century

Cortés (Hernán) – the leader of the Spanish Conquistadors, who arrived in Tenochtitlan with Spanish soldiers in 1519

Festivals – special days of celebration, usually a holiday when everyone would join in the festivities

Glyph – a picture sign making up the Aztec system of picture writing

Guild – organization, like a modern trade union, made up of workers of the same craft

Mixtec – an early civilization living in what is now called Mexico around 1200 B.C.

Montezuma – the Emperor who ruled the Aztec Empire at the time of the Spanish Conquest

Mosaic – a work of art made from tiny pieces of precious stones or shell, carefully pieced together

Nomadic – wandering with no fixed home

Prophecy – a story or legend that predicts what will happen in the future

Quetzal – a tropical bird, highly prized by the Aztecs for its beautiful plumage and tail feathers

Relief – a design which is raised above, or cut into, its background

Ritual – a ceremony, with special prayers and actions, performed as an offering to the gods

Sacrifice – an offering, sometimes animal or human, made to please the gods; the Aztecs believed that if the sacrifices stopped, the world would come to an end

Scribe – professional writer and record keeper, who could read and write the Aztec system of picture writing

Superstitious – believing in good luck and bad omens

Tenochtitlan – the name of the ancient Aztec capital city, known today as Mexico City

Textiles – all cloth and fabric, either woven or non-woven, made from yarn or fibers

Tortillas – a flat pancake, made from ground corn kneaded into a dough and cooked – still eaten in Mexico today

Tribute – the payment of valuable goods to the Aztecs by their conquered neighbors; if they stopped paying tribute, it would lead to war